Paleo Made Easy

Gluten Free, Wheat Free, Sugar Free Cookbook

Contents

About the Book

For all Paleo diet followers this book is written to make your life easier. The hardest part of a diet can be the time and energy it takes to plan ahead. Sticking to any eating plan requires stocking up and being prepared. These recipes are all fast to prepare, easy and some you can take on the go. Don't fall victim to the convenience of fast foods. In this book you will find a variety of fresh delicious salads, easy to set and forget crockpot recipes and snacks to go.

Introduction

The Paleo diet follows the eating habits of our Paleolithic ancestors who lived 10,000 years ago. They ate what they could hunt or gather from the natural environment and ate it in its natural form. Research has shown that eating along these guidelines show health benefit that are significantly increased over the standard American diet. Adherers to the diet have shown weight loss, reduced blood pressure, cardiovascular health, healthy blood pressure and healthy blood sugar levels.

The foods included in Paleo eating include seafood, meat, fruits, vegetables and nuts. Some common foods on the no-no list are refined carbohydrates and sugar, processed foods and gluten containing foods. By replacing low nutrient foods with nutrient dense foods the body can begin to repair cellular and intestinal damage. Get back to basics with these delicious easy and fast recipes to make Paleo eating convenient, healthy and tasty.

Salads

Hawaiian Pork Salad

Serves 4-6

3 lbs. pork shoulder (bone left in)

4 garlic cloves

1 yellow or white onion (thin sliced)

1 tsp. garlic powder

¼ tsp. sea salt

2 romaine lettuce heads (chopped)

1 red bell pepper (diced)

4 oz. mushrooms (thin sliced)

2 c. pineapple (diced)

½ c. pepperoni (diced)

2 tbsp. coconut oil

Begin by placing your onions, garlic and pork shoulder into a crockpot, then coat with garlic powder and salt. Place the lid on your crockpot and let cook for eight hours, then, shred the meat with a fork. After shredding your meat, sauté your mushrooms on medium heat in coconut oil. Next, in a large bowl, combine your ingredients with the cooked pork and toss to incorporate. Serve and enjoy!

Chef Salad

Serves 2

4 large eggs (hardboiled)

1 red-leaf lettuce head (chopped)

½ lb. grilled chicken breast (cut to small cubes)

2 bacon slices (crisped and crumbled)

8 cherry tomatoes (cut in half)

4 green onions (thin sliced)

2 celery stalks (diced)

1 avocado (pitted and diced)

Begin by cooking your bacon on medium heat in a skillet until it is crisp and crumbly. Next grill your chicken thoroughly and then cut to equal sized cubes. Chop your lettuce and toss all of your ingredients together and serve! Top with Simple Salad Dressing.

Cabbage & Pineapple Salad

Serves 1-2

½ head red cabbage (shredded)

½ pineapple (peeled and diced)

1 c. hazelnuts (chopped)

Begin by shredding your cabbage and dicing the pineapple. Toss together in a bowl and top with chopped hazelnuts, enjoy!

Fajita Salad

Serves 2

1 tbsp. melted coconut oil

½ yellow onion (diced)

¾ lb. chicken breast (boneless and skinless)

½ tsp. cumin (ground)

2 tsp. dried oregano

¼ tsp. sea salt

1 red or green bell pepper (chopped)

1 head red leaf lettuce (chopped) or romaine

2 fresh tomatoes (diced)

1 avocado

Begin by heating a skillet over medium heat and sautéing your onions in coconut oil. When the onions become translucent, add in your cumin, salt, oregano and chicken and cook thoroughly being sure to stir often. When the chicken has cooked through and begins to brown, throw in your peppers and continue to cook until soft. Divide your lettuce into two separate plate and top with your ingredients, enjoy!

Chicken & Kale Salad

Serves 2

6 c. kale (chopped)

2 tbsp. extra virgin olive oil

1 fresh lemon (juiced)

1/8 tsp. sea salt

¼ tsp. fresh ground pepper

2 chicken breasts (skinned, cooked and sliced)

Begin by washing your kale and removing any stems, then thin slice. Use a large bowl to toss you kale in lemon juice, olive oil, salt and pepper and coat thoroughly. Top with cooked chicken breast and serve.

Indian Style Slaw

Serves 2-3

1 green cabbage head (chopped fine)

3 red tomatoes (diced)

1 c. shredded coconut (unsweetened)

½ c. almond flour (sifted)

1 large date (soaked and mashed)

1 lemon (juiced)

2 tbsp. olive oil

½ tsp. mustard seed (ground)

½ tsp. cumin seeds (ground)

¼ tsp. turmeric (powder)

¼ tsp. sea salt

Start by tossing your tomatoes, almond flour, cabbage and coconut oil together in a large bowl and then set to the side for later. Next use a small bowl to mash your soaked date, then stir in the remaining ingredients to make a dressing. Toss your salad in your homemade dressing to coat well and serve!

Tuna Salad (Spicy)

Serves 2-3

12 oz. of tuna

1 c. black olives (chopped)

2 green onions (chopped)

1 jalapeno (thin sliced)

3 tbsp. capers

½ tsp. red chili (flaked or powder)

2 lemons (juiced)

1 head butter lettuce (chopped)

1 avocado (sliced and pitted)

Begin by combining all of your ingredients, except the lettuce, in a large bowl and tossing well. Prepare a bed of lettuce and pour your ingredients on top. Top with fresh sliced avocado before serving, enjoy!

Paleo Taco Salad

Serves 2

1 lb. ground beef (turkey works too)

2 tbsp. chili powder

1 tsp. garlic salt

1 tsp. cumin (powder)

½ tsp. dried oregano

½ tsp. sea salt

¾ c. water (filtered)

½ yellow onion (diced)

1 red tomato (diced)

3 romaine hearts

1 can black olives

1 avocado

1 small jar of salsa

Begin by cooking your beef (or turkey) and onion in a skillet on medium heat. Cook for three minutes, then add in your garlic salt, cumin, chili powder, oregano, water and salt and let cook for another five minutes. Next tear your lettuce into pieces and place on two separate plates. Top with your cooked meat, avocado, tomatoes, cilantro, salsa and olives. Enjoy!

Apple Slaw

Serves 1-2

½ head cabbage (chopped)

1 green apple (grated)

1 celery stalk (chopped)

1 red bell pepper (chopped)

¼ c. olive oil

1 lemon (juiced)

2 tbsp. raw honey

1 tsp. celery seed

¼ tsp. sea salt

Use a large bowl to toss your apple, bell pepper, cabbage and celery together and set to the side. Next use a small bowl to whisk your remaining ingredients together until well mixed. Now top your salad with the homemade dressing, toss and enjoy!

Tomato Salsa Salad

Serves 1-2

1 cilantro bunch (chopped)

4 Roma tomatoes (diced)

1 red onion (diced)

1 chili pepper (fine diced)

1 black avocado (diced)

1 tbsp. olive oil

¼ tsp. sea salt

Begin by tossing all of your ingredients together in a large bowl to combine well. Top your salad with diced avocado, serve and enjoy!

Orange Salad

Serves 2

2 large oranges (peeled and segmented)

1 large avocado (pitted and diced)

¼ c. cashews (chopped)

3 handfuls of spinach

Drizzle of olive oil

Sea salt & black pepper (as needed)

6 oz. chicken breast (cooked and sliced)

Begin by peeling and segmenting your orange and then set to the side. Next split your greens up onto two separate plates and top with segmented orange, cashews and avocado. Top with olive oil and sliced chicken breast and serve.

Cauliflower Salad

Serves 2-3

1 head cauliflower (chopped to small pieces)

2 celery stalks (diced)

¼ yellow onion (fine diced)

1 tbsp. parsley (chopped)

2 large eggs (hardboiled and diced)

2 tbsp. mayonnaise

1 tbsp. mustard

½ tsp. sea salt

Begin by steaming your cauliflower on the stove-top under medium heat, until a mushy texture is achieved. When done steaming, remove from the heat, rinse with cold water and place in a large bowl. Next stir in the remaining ingredients and toss to coat everything evenly, serve and enjoy.

Spinach Salad

Serves 1-2

1 handful of fresh spinach

4 green onions (chopped)

1 lemon (juiced)

2 tbs. olive oil

¼ tbsp. fresh pepper (ground)

Begin by washing and chopping your fresh spinach and placing in a medium sized mixing bowl. Add in your lemon juice, olive oil, green onions and pepper, toss well to incorporate and serve.

Crockpot

Slow Cooked Shredded Beef

Serves 4-6

3 lbs. sirloin steak

2 yellow onions (peeled and sliced)

½ c. chicken broth (or beef)

1 tsp. sea salt

1 tsp. garlic powder

½ tsp. paprika

½ tsp. black pepper

¼ tsp. white pepper

¼ tsp. chili powder

Place the onions in the bottom of your crockpot and place the meat on top. Evenly coat everything in spices and place the lid on. Set to low heat and cook for eight hours. Shred the meat with a fork after eight hours and then cover and cook for another two hours.

Green Chili Pork

Serves 2-4

2 lbs. pork roast

1 yellow onion (chopped)

2 garlic cloves (minced)

4 oz. green chili (diced)

2 Anaheim chili (deseeded and chopped)

1 poblano pepper (deseeded and chopped)

1 jalapeño pepper (diced)

2 c. chicken broth

8oz. tomatoes (diced)

1 tsp. oregano

1 tsp. sea salt

1 tsp. white pepper

½ tsp. cumin

½ tsp. sage

½ tsp. paprika

½ tsp. cayenne pepper

Begin by placing your roast into the crockpot and surround with veggies. Next, pour in the tomatoes and green chili and top with spices. Now pour in your broth, being careful not to wash all the spices off. Set your crockpot to low and cook for six hours. After six hours of cook time, shred your pork with a fork and then set to cook for another hour or two.

Cauliflower Rice & Garlic Pork

Serves 4-6

2 lbs. pork roast

6 garlic cloves (peeled)

2 heads of cauliflower (chopped)

1 chicken broth

1 tsp. ground cumin

1 tsp. sea salt

½ tsp. black pepper

Begin by placing the cauliflower into your food processor and shred to a rice like consistency. Next, place your "rice" in the crockpot and cover in broth. Stir the salt and pepper into the "rice" solution and then toss in your garlic cloves. Place your pork roast on top of the "rice" and set to low for eight hours to cook. When done cooking, shred your pork and stir everything up in the pot. Serve and enjoy!

Ginger Apple Shredded Pork

Serves 4-6

2 lbs. pork roast

1 yellow onion (peeled and sliced)

2 red apples (sliced)

⅔ c. beef broth (could also use filtered water)

1 tbsp. raw honey

2 tbsp. fresh ginger (grated)

1 tsp. cinnamon (ground)

1 tsp. salt

½ tsp. paprika

½ tsp. black pepper

2 garlic cloves (peeled and minced)

1 bay leave

Place all of your ingredients into the crockpot and stir well to incorporate. Next set the heat to low and cook for ten hours. Shred your pork with a fork and serve.

Crockpot Chicken & Spinach

Serves 2-4

2 lbs. chicken thighs

½ c. balsamic vinegar

6 cloves garlic (peeled and minced)

2 tsp. oregano

2 tsp. Italian parsley

¼ tbsp. black pepper

10 oz. baby spinach

Begin by mixing all of your ingredients together in a small bowl and whisking thoroughly. Then place the chicken into your crockpot and pour the ingredient mix over the top. Set to low and cook for six hours, serve hot!

Italian Roast

Serves 4-6

3 tbsp. olive oil

3 lbs. beef roast (boneless)

1 sweet onion (diced)

14 oz. tomatoes (diced)

5 garlic cloves (minced)

1 tbsp. oregano

1 tsp. rosemary

1 tsp. Italian parsley

½ c. red wine

Begin by placing your roast in the crockpot. Next surround the roast with your garlic, onion and tomatoes. Now coat the top of the roast and veggies with the remaining ingredients and set to low for ten hours. Let cool for five minutes before serving.

Sweet Potato Chili

Serves 2-4

1 lb. ground beef

2 sweet potatoes (peeled and chopped)

½ white onion (chopped)

1 green bell pepper (chopped)

2 garlic cloves (chopped)

1½ tbsp. chili powder

1 tsp. cumin

½ tsp. black pepper

¼ tsp. sea salt

14 oz. tomatoes (diced)

2 c. beef broth

1 c. water (filtered)

Begin by browning your beef in a large skillet on medium heat. When browned on all sides, drain off half of the fat and put the rest along with the beef into the crockpot. Place the remaining ingredients into the crockpot and stir well to mix it up. Set your crockpot on low and cook for six hours.

Oil & Herb Whole Chicken

Serves 4-5

1 whole chicken (4 lbs. is a good size)

1 c. olive oil

3 tbsp. oregano

3 tbsp. thyme

First place the chicken in the crockpot. Cover in olive oil, thyme and oregano and set to low of r eight to ten hours. When done cooking, divide to pieces and serve.

Snacks

Fruit Roll-ups

Serves 2-4

2 large red apples

2 c. fresh strawberries

1 tsp. cinnamon (ground)

¼ c. water (filtered)

Begin by coring and dicing your red apples. Then place your strawberries, apples, cinnamon and water in to a blender and puree for thirty seconds until smooth. Pour your puree onto a plastic sheet and place in the dehydrator for eight hours. When the time has expired, remove from the heat and let air dry for another four hours.

Sweet Banana Treat

Serves 2

1 large banana (very ripe)

2 tbsp. almond butter (unsweetened)

2 tbsp. whole coconut milk

Shredded coconut

Begin by slicing your banana equally into two small bowls. Top each bowl with almond butter and coconut milk and stir slightly to incorporate. Sprinkle shredded coconut on top and enjoy.

Salmon Poppers

Serves 3

2 endive heads

4 oz. fresh salmon

½ red onion (minced)

½ avocado (pitted and sliced)

¼ tsp. sea salt

¼ tsp. fresh ground black pepper

1 tbsp. olive oil

Start by washing your endive leaves and then separate into three bowls in equal amounts. Top the endive with red onion, salmon and avocado. Sprinkle with salt and pepper and a drizzle of olive oil, enjoy.

Shrimp Cocktail

Serves 2-3

1 lb. shrimp (shelled)

6 tbsp. chili sauce

2 tbsp. lemon juice

½ tbsp. horse-radish

1 tsp. fresh onion (grated)

1 celery stalk (fine chopped)

4 lettuce leaves

Begin by boiling two quarts of water in a medium sized pot on high heat. Add in the shrimp and let cook for five minutes. When done cooking, remove the shrimp from the boiling water and rinse quickly in cold water. Set the shrimp to the side in a bowl and then whisk together your lemon juice, chili and onion together. Toss your shrimp in the sauce and then top with celery and salad greens.

Trail Mix

Serves 2

1 c. whole almonds

½ c. whole cashews

½ c. raw pumpkin seeds

½ c. raw sunflower seeds

½ c. raisins

½ c. dried currants

½ c. dried blueberries (or cranberries)

Combine your ingredients together in an airtight Tupperware or bag and shake to combine well. Store your leftovers in the same airtight container.

Salami Stacks

Serves 2

¼ lb. hard salami (thin sliced)

Mustard

1 c. cherry tomatoes (cut in half)

Layer your salami with mustard between in stacks of four. Top each stack with a cherry tomato half and enjoy!

Apple Chips

Serves 2

2 c. apple juice (unsweetened)

1 cinnamon stick

2 large red apples (cored and sliced)

Cinnamon (ground)

Begin by heating a large pot on high heat, then pour in your apple juice and cinnamon stick. Bring to a low boil and then slowly add in your apple slices. Boil the slices for five minutes until they appear translucent, then remove from the juice and pat dry. Place your slices on a wire rack and then place in the oven at 250 degrees for thirty-five minutes. Your slices should now be crisp and crunchy, enjoy!

Kale Chips

Serves 2

1 bunch kale

1 tsp. olive oil

¼ tsp. sea salt

First, wash your kale and remove any remaining stems. Next cut your kale into three inch sections and lay flat on a large baking sheet. Cover the kale in a light coat of olive oil and sea salt. Place in the oven at 350 degrees for fifteen minutes until the kale is crisp and then enjoy while hot.

Deviled Eggs w/ Guacamole

Serves 4-6

4 large eggs (hard-boiled)

1 black avocado

2 tsp. hot sauce

1 tsp. fresh lemon juice

¼ tsp. sea salt

½ tsp. fresh ground pepper

Start off by peeling your hardboiled eggs, then cut in half lengthwise and remove the yokes. Next mash the yolks together with hot sauce, lemon juice and avocado. Season your mix with salt and pepper and the spoon the eggs halves full.

Ant Logs

Serves 2

2 celery stalks

4 tbsp. cashew butter (or almond butter)

2 tbsp. raisins

Wash celery. Spread cashew (or almond) butter on each stalk and top with a layer of raisins. Serve.

Printed in Dunstable, United Kingdom

73606348R00022